FREEHO
SEASIDE PLOTS

THE 'OLD DUTCH ISLAND'

20 Miles only from Fenchurch Street   Good Train Service   Cheap Rates

F. W. B. HESTER

Every WEDNESDAY and THURSDAY

500 PLOTS
OF VALUABLE

FREEHOLD BUILDING LAND

Oyster Fleet & Shell Beach Estates, Canvey-on-Sea, Essex,

This Land will in the course of a very short period greatly increase in value and at the present time affords a splendid opportunity to both large and small buyers.   Several of the Estates are already developing

WINTER GARDENS, ELECTRIC RAILWAY, PIER, Etc.

Every facility is offered to Visitors and Holiday Seekers

BUNGALOWS and REFRESHMENTS on very reasonable terms by the
WEEK, MONTH or QUARTER

Bracing Air.   Good Fishing, Shooting, Boating & Bathing.

10 per cent gives immediate possession

Free Deeds. .. Easy Payments.

FREE RAILWAY VOUCHERS to attend the Land Sale and
View the Estates can be obtained of the Auctioneer

F W B HESTER, 145, Fenchurch Street, E.C. or
The VENDOR, Estate Office, Canvey-on-Sea, Essex, and also at the
No 4 Platform Barrier Fenchurch Street Railway Station

CANVEY ISLAND
A Pictorial History

Best wishes

The 14-Star Tea Gardens.

CANVEY ISLAND
A Pictorial History

Geoff Barsby

Phillimore

1992

Published by
PHILLIMORE & CO. LTD.,
Shopwyke Hall, Chichester, Sussex

© Geoff Barsby, 1992

ISBN 0 85033 846 8

Printed and bound in Great Britain by
BIDDLES LTD.,
Guildford, Surrey

List of Illustrations

Frontispiece: The 14-Star Tea Gardens

Illustration Acknowledgements

Many thanks to the following for the loan of postcards and photographs and permission to reproduce them here: Nora Bishop, 37, 129; the Cox family, 59, 82, 110, 154; Essex Record Office, 8; Essex Police Museum, 23; Albert Jones, 62, 162; Mrs. Joseph (née Alterman), 151 Mrs. Stevens and family, 75, 117.

Preface

Having been deeply interested in local history for a number of years, an avid member of the Canvey Historical and Conservation Society, and author and publisher of *Years Gone By* magazine, I have been approached many times to 'come out' in hardback.

I hope therefore that I have managed to do justice to all those kind people who have provided much encouragement. At this point I feel I should mention in particular the assistance I have received on dates and information on sitings from Margaret Payne and Vic Went, friends and longstanding members of the Historical and Conservation Society.

Canvey Island has always had a reputation for being a close-knit community, and no-one is more certain of that than I am. Having been born there and knowing the people as I do, remembering those who have given their all to it, now sadly passed on, such as Aubrey Stevens and Fred McCave, I am proud to be part of a community which helps and befriends its neighbours.

In this portrayal of Canvey I have selected what I consider to be the most important periods of its history, from the Roman and Dutch occupations to the modern day, ending with the floods of 1953.

For a place that is steeped in nostalgic interest and superstition, and has its fair share of ghostly stories, it leaves more for discovery and perhaps another book.

Introduction

The Five Isles of Cana's People

Like many of the place-names in the area, the name of Canvey can be traced back to the Anglo-Saxons, and carries the meaning 'The Island of Cana's People'.

Originally the island was made up of five separate islands, and maps exist which show this. Moreover, there are archaeological theories that suggest Canvey was once part of the mainland. Its coarse marshlands were known for the excellence of their pasture and the large flocks of sheep they were able to sustain – the fat-tailed variety being the favoured breed.

Long before Canvey became an ecclesiastical parish in 1881, it came under the possession of a man called Swein. It is unclear how the division of Canvey into separate parishes came about, though it is likely that it occurred during the reign of Henry II. Swein's grandson, Henry de Essex, was accused of cowardice, and all his land was confiscated by the crown. Swein had also acquired 55 other manors in Essex, including Thundersley, Benfleet, Hadleigh, Rayleigh, Rochford and Prittlewell. The land was subsequently redistributed by the king, much of it being bestowed as gifts to those in the king's favour. This was possibly the beginning of parish ownership. The island's nine parishes belonged to Bowers Gifford, Hadleigh, Laindon, Leigh, North and South Benfleet, Pitsea, Prittlewell, Southchurch and Vange. The parishes were not divided into uniform shapes as the boundaries were natural barriers such as the curves of drainage channels, rather than fences.

Canvey Island is not mentioned by name in Domesday Book, although much stress is laid upon the coastal marshes south of Essex, which are estimated to have provided grazing for 18,000 sheep. Numerous references were made to the marshes held by several manors situated near the coast as detached portions of inland manors.

Sheep farming was a thriving industry. Not only were the wool and meat important but the ewes' milk was made into cheese. London, so easily reached by sea and river, presented a ready market for such produce. Until the first sea defences were erected, the shepherds were the only inhabitants on the island, and they must have led a hard and lonely existence. It would appear that their only shelters were the wicks where the cheese-making took place. With the constant flooding from frequent high tides it would seem that the shepherds safeguarded their flocks and wicks by building earth hillocks on which to protect them. They may have taken the idea for this directly from watching the sheep on the south of the island, for they would always climb to the safety of the Red Hills as the flood tides threatened. It was these sites which later became the areas upon which farmhouses were built, hence the appropriately named Hill Hall Farm.

Much of the Thames-side marshlands suffered from gradual subsidence, and there is evidence that, from the 14th century onwards, owners of the coastal areas were forced to build barriers around their property in order to protect it from the tides. The new enclosures were of horseshoe shape and generally added to existing walls or mainland.

They were built periodically, to form part of the island's first sea-defence. When new enclosures were needed they were often placed in front of the existing wall, materials from the older structure frequently being used for the new. This was eventually forbidden, since it came to be realised that the old, or 'counter walls', as they were known, formed a useful second line of defence should the outer wall be breached. Thus a fairly uniform type of enclosure fronting the River Thames was formed, which was mistakenly thought to have been constructed by the Romans in a single building operation.

Landholdings on the island gradually changed hands, and in the reign of Edward II the acquisition of land by John de Apeton (thought to be an ancestor of Sir Roger Appulton) occurred. The marshes of Northwick-cum-Wykes, Chaffleet and Fatherwick subsequently came under his ownership. By 1557 the marshes of Northwick and Westwick had also come into the family's possession, making it one of the principal landowners on the island. The other major landowning family was the Bakers, who held Knightswyke, Southwyke and Attenmarsh.

Although frequent attempts had been made by the islanders to overcome the constant invasion by the sea, it was Sir Henry Appleton who enlisted the help of the Dutch. The reclamation of Canvey may have been due to the suggestion of Joas Croppenburg, a wealthy Dutch haberdasher of Cheapside and an acquaintance of Appleton. There were certain similarities between Canvey's problems and those of the Netherlands.

A Dutch engineer, Cornelius Vermuyden, commissioned to drain the Fens, was related by marriage to Croppenburg. Vermuyden is first mentioned in England as being employed to repair a breach in the sea wall at Dagenham. It seems unlikely that he travelled to England solely to complete such a minor task, and his work at Dagenham was more probably a stop-gap to his negotiations for the more involved work to come.

His payment for the work is interesting, since the Havering Commission, which had been his employer at Dagenham, paid not in cash but by a grant of land. This method of payment would have appealed greatly to the Dutch, for it allowed them to enjoy a standing within the community which they would not have achieved so easily in their homeland. The Dutch were already taking an interest in settling in southern England, and were particularly prevalent around the marshland areas. Julius Sludder was a Dutchman who by 1622 already owned part of Canvey, and may have been responsible for the building of the Dutch cottage in 1618.

When it was proposed that Canvey be reclaimed from the encroachments of the sea, an agreement was made between the island's landowners – Sir Henry Appleton, Julius Sludder, John, William and Mary Blackmore, Abigail Baker, and Thomas Binckes and his wife – and Joas Croppenburg. Croppenburg would be responsible for financing the project and, in return for a fee, one-third of all lands recovered and made safe would go to him. This agreement was made a decree of the Court of Chancery on 27 February 1623, with the stipulation that the agreement be made void should any breaches in the sea walls remain unrepaired within a year of their being built. The name of Cornelius Vermuyden did not appear on the agreement, even though he was instrumental in the work. There is no indication of how the 300 workmen brought over from Holland were paid, though it may be supposed that some at least in part were given a land grant. Here we may have the reason for the existence of the early Dutch community.

Though the scheme was financed by Joas Croppenburg, it is clear that he borrowed on the security of the Third Acre Lands, as they became known. This capital probably came from Holland, for in 1637 Heinrick Brouwer wrote from Amsterdam of his claim to a sixteenth share in Canvey Island, acquired through his acquaintance in 1622 with Croppenburg.

The Dutch were responsible for the maintenance of the sea walls on the Third Acre Lands, and it must have been an expense that was difficult to cover. It was also a bone of contention between them and the private landowners on the island. Whilst the Dutch ploughed their profits into repair work, as surety against losing their land, the Freelanders were not bound to maintain their property in a similar way. It may have been this that led the Dutch gradually to move away from the area, some returning to the Netherlands and others selling their property in exchange for other property that did not require as much work. Whatever the cause, the wall was left to deteriorate.

In 1791 came 'outrageous tides', where the damage to the defences was so severe that landowners had to advance money for immediate repairs, for fear of losing the whole island. It was this that led the landowners to petition Parliament in 1792 with an act for 'effectually embanking, draining and otherwise improving the Island of Canvey in the County of Essex'. The act established a board of 24 Commissioners of Sewers for the island. Like many similar bodies of commissioners they had special powers and responsibilities of their own. The commissioners recognised that, although the maintenance to the walls of the Third Acre Lands legally fell upon the owners, the task was beyond their capabilities. The commissioners made provision for new insets behind the existing wall, where the breaches had occurred. In this way, the old wall and the marshlands between would serve as an extra defence against the tides. This protection was added to the south of the island, where a considerable amount of the old Dutch wall was 'flung to sea'.

During 1792 and 1812 wall rates were levied on both the owners of Freelands and Third Acre properties and, at such times that repairs could not be met, a loan was arranged from the Freelands tax to Third Acre. In subsequent years, when profit would arise after outlay from Third Acre land, the loan would be repaid.

On 18 January 1881 a flood caused immense damage to a stretch of wall from Scarhouse to Leigh Beck. Five hundred men, including 150 soldiers, were employed to repair the wall before the danger of Spring tides. Under the provisions of the 1792 act it was exceedingly difficult to raise enough money for repair work, and so a further act was passed, which included a tax on Outsands (privately reclaimed lands standing outside the old Dutch wall). This in no way changed the original historical implications of the Third Acre Lands.

More flooding occurred in November 1897. Lasting for a number of weeks it caused severe damage to farmers' crops. On top of an already severe agricultural depression, the increase in sea-wall taxes caused many of the island's farmers to sell out, often at a very low price.

The commissioners were always concerned about the deterioration of the wall. One of the first actions to be taken by the newly formed body of commissioners was to order a notice to be given publicly, 'that all persons who shall take away the cockle shells from off the banks, saltings, or any part of the Island ... be prosecuted'. The shells, found in great quantity, particularly around the Leigh Beck area were used in cement, and could be found in the walls of Hadleigh Castle and Canvey's Dutch cottages, as well as forming the linings of ditches and the surfacing of paths.

Roman Connection

Canvey's history goes back much further than the Dutch, to Roman and possibly even Celtic occupation.

Many pieces of pre-Roman and Roman pottery have been uncovered during building works on Canvey. However, the fragments of late-Celtic pottery have been discovered near to the surface and in the sand on parts of the seashore, so it is difficult to ascertain whether the Celts actually lived here. It is more likely that these pieces were washed ashore during the constant flooding of the time. As it would seem that no other evidence exists to connect the Celts with the island, any occupation that took place was for a brief period only. Not so vague, however, is the evidence of the Romans and their interest in the island's natural resources.

Numerous pieces of crude red pottery have been discovered on the island, consistent with the type of soil found on the island's Red Hills. These mounds, found in all parts of Essex, consist of a type of burnt earth, loose in texture and of varying shades of red. There is little to distinguish them to the eye, as they are often similar to the marsh mounds nearby, but excavation yields their varying colour and composition.

The possibility that pottery was the main reason for Roman activity in Canvey is remote, since no major kiln workings have been discovered. It is reasonable to believe, therefore, that the pottery was not so much an industry but a purely domestic feature of Roman habitation.

It is more likely that the Romans' main interest was in the production of salt, which was a vital and necessary commodity of the time. A great deal of importance was placed in the curing of fish and meat; this idea is supported by the findings of salt water evaporation vessels. When studied by the eminent Dr. Sorby, the coastline and creeks of Essex were pronounced to be very suitable in salt content, and of considerable value for salt evaporation, particularly during the summer time.

The discovery of vessels for storage and for carrying brine to other encampments, along with evaporation pots, lends evidence to the theory that pottery was a secondary trade. Fragments of pottery can still be unearthed today, the cruder type supposedly manufactured locally, whilst the more refined pieces, not having the same connection with the industry, are thought to have been made elsewhere. The suggestion has been made that these finer pieces, particularly those found around Dead Man's Point, may have been made for burial purposes. That area of Canvey was once raised above sea-level and could well have been used as a Roman burial ground. This theory would help to explain why fragments of pottery were washed up in this area and found at low tide.

Traces of the Past

We know with certainty that Roman occupation left its mark. Amateur archaeologists are often to be seen at the eastern end of the island, arousing fresh interest with their finds. Fragments of pottery have been pieced together, to create an entire bowl, which the Keeper of Antiquities at Southend has identified as Samian-ware. Other digs have uncovered several urns, one of which appeared to be a cremation urn, complete with bones inside, more than 2,000 years old. This discovery furthered the idea that there could be a burial site on the island, a theory which had never occurred before.

One never knows what could be discovered next on the island, and perhaps we should not be too hasty in throwing away what appears to be an old piece of metal protruding between our lines of cabbages! In 1989 a local archaeologist uncovered a 2,000-year-old bronze bracelet. Its design was crude, but its discovery momentous, and what a conversation piece!

Canvey's Cheese Industry

In its early days Canvey, sometimes referred to as Canwaie Iles, had a thriving dairy industry. It has been recorded that in 1592 some 4,000 sheep were on the island. It is but also over to Southend. As Hester mapped out his vision of a grand promenade adjacent to a pier, bandstands and a Kursaal to match that at Southend, customers must frequently have fallen under his spell.

To his credit, he had built the most spectacular of Winter Gardens on Canvey, intended to cover an area of six square miles when it was completed. The glass conservatories not only housed exotic plants and fruits – peacocks strutted amongst other birds, whilst gold- and silver-coloured fish swam in ponds and under fountains.

Hester also laid a metal mono-rail tramway to carry trippers through the gardens: past the colourful foliage, the full-size statuettes, the refreshment area, Dutch bazaar and the shopping alcoves. He took every advantage of the Dutch heritage of the area, encouraging the wearing of the Dutch national costume in many of his schemes. Hester also made up, and took full responsibility for the Dutch names given to many of the older roads on the island.

'Nothing ventured, nothing gained', was a maxim Hester appeared to live by. His ideas for the project extended to a Venetian canal, with gondolas making their way through the interior waters of the island. So convinced was Hester that Canvey would boom under his patronage, that he allowed his enthusiasm for new schemes to overstretch his pocket, which led to his bankruptcy in 1905.

The Great Divide
There can be no doubt that the construction of the first real bridge to the mainland was of enormous importance to the future development of Canvey. The Colvin Bridge was named after the Lord Lieutenant of Essex, Brigadier-General R. B. Colvin, C.B., who performed the pile driving ceremony on 21 May 1930. The bridge was officially opened exactly a year later, on 21 May 1931, by Alderman J. H. Burrows.

The provision of a swing bridge had frequently been requested by the Rev. Hayes before his death in 1900. The idea was not taken up again seriously until December 1929, and it was eventually sanctioned by the Ministry of Transport in March 1930. It was estimated to have cost £15,000; since the population of the island was quite small it was agreed that the Treasury should meet a significant part of the cost, and they contributed £9,263 towards it.

Before the building of the bridge, the only means of crossing to or from the mainland was by ferry, or stepping stones at low tide. Whenever possible visits were arranged around the tide-tables and these were published by local papers and council guidebooks.

Two punts and two row-boats represented the ferry, being on duty all hours of day and night. If an emergency presented itself at an awkward hour, there was a bell which, if rung loud enough, caused the ferryman to come running from his nearby cottage. Passengers paid 1d. for the trip, later raised to 1½d. For 2d. passengers could take their bicycles across.

Crossing the creek posed a problem for animals and large vehicles; cows and horses had a tendency to be swept away from their drivers in unguarded moments whilst making the crossing. Cars, coal waggons and carts were sometimes abandoned when the journey had been left too late and the incoming tide had caught the drivers unawares. It was not surprising, then, that there were parties all over the island when the bridge was opened – the day was even declared a local holiday. Foot passengers and cars lined up to follow Alderman Burrows and his entourage from the Canvey Chamber of Trade over the bridge.

The Colvin swing bridge continued to give preference to river traffic, mainly fully-loaded sailing barges. It was used for the last time on 26 November 1968, and was finally demolished in February 1973, when the present bridge replaced it.

The Chapman Lighthouse

After more than a century of use, a short ceremony was held to say 'goodbye' to the Chapman lighthouse before it was demolished in 1957. The lighthouse, with its clockwork mechanism came into operation in 1851, four years after a lightship had been moored in the area.

For centuries the perilous off-shore mud-flats had claimed many victims. The Romans are thought to have devised some form of beacon as a warning in the area. It was not until the 19th century that pressure was brought to bear on Trinity House by a group of shipowners, registering the need for a permanent signal. Taking into account the unstable condition of the riverbed, James Walker, the consultant lighthouse engineer to Trinity House at that time, drew up a unique design for a pile lighthouse made entirely of iron. Walker also supervised its construction.

The hexagonal-shaped living accommodation for the lighthouse keeper and his assistant was somewhat spartan, comprising a living room, bedroom, kitchen-cum-washroom and storeroom. For the purpose of going ashore a rowing boat was suspended from the side of the lighthouse.

The salt water eventually took its toll and the lighthouse became in danger of collapse. Today in its place, bobbing 800 yards off-shore, is a single bell-buoy. No doubt it does the job, but is considered by many to be a far less attractive guardian.

The Floods of 1953 ... They believed it would never happen again

Though the Dutch reclamation work of the 17th century brought some security from the ravages of the sea, the sea walls were frequently breached. In 1883 the Canvey Sea Defences Act was passed, which updated an earlier act of Parliament. The act of 1883 empowered a body of commissioners to levy rates from owners of the outsands in the same way as their neighbours. The money gathered was not only spent on the upkeep of the walls, but also on their improvement – the commissioning body had the walls raised and levelled, extending them on the Thames front to a height of 2ft. above the highest tide level. In January 1888, however, valuable land slipped into the sea. Nine years later, on 29 November 1897, a high tide submerged part of Canvey. This led to research by the Meteorological Office and other institutes into the possibility of accurately predicting floods.

The highest recorded levels of the 1938 tides indicated that the defences were still too low, although fortunately no serious floods occurred.

New-found confidence in the defences inspired an entry in the *Canvey Island Official Guide* of 1949: 'The valuable and arduous work of the Canvey Island Sea Wall Commission, who keeps a vigilant eye on the present works, render such a thing very, very unlikely now'. Then came the storms of 1953. Due to the effects of the unrelenting and violent force 12 northerly winds, a surge of water began driving southward when nothing more than the usual Spring tide had been predicted. Flood alert warnings were sent out by Scotland Yard to the City of London police, in accordance with plans formulated after the floods of 1928. All coastal areas were on stand-by, although no-one could have guessed the full extent of the sea's fury. Messages were relayed as to the worsening conditions, and at about 1 a.m. on 1 February the island's walls were breached, with disastrous results. Under a plan termed Operation King Canute the fire brigade were sent out to alert the people of Canvey. At the same time the siren and fire maroons were sounded in such a way that it was hoped islanders would become curious enough to get out of bed to look outside. Fortunately some did and were evacuated, others were too deep in sleep to hear anything above the howling winds. They either woke up much later when the icy water lapped over them, or sadly never woke at all. Although lives were lost all along the coast that night, Canvey suffered the worst, with 58 people dying in the floods. For the survivors, cold, bleak hours, huddled in a loft, or worse perhaps on a roof, barely above sea-level, ensured that it was a night not to be forgotten.

The rescued became refugees, transported to hastily set-up rest centres, mostly in schools and church halls in the area. Benfleet primary school was the first to open its doors, though it was grossly inadequate to cope with the enormous numbers; nevertheless it bore the brunt of the early hours admirably. An appeal for aid brought kindhearted responses from around the country, with great quantities of clothes, food and sweets being donated. A visit by Queen Elizabeth, the Queen Mother, and the young Princess Margaret provided sympathy and encouragement.

Back on the island, a mobile dispensary took care of animal casualties, with three animal organisations, the R.S.P.C.A., O.D.F.L. and the P.D.S.A. giving assistance. At the same time Civil Defence workers and volunteers joined with the Army and Royal Air Force to make temporary repairs to the walls. The Women's Voluntary Service took care of the food for the crews working on the walls. The repairs were urgent, since the next wave of high tides was due within a fortnight.

Victims of the floods stayed with friends and relatives, or in some cases accepted the hospitality of complete strangers, until it was time to go back to the island. On return every tenant was supplied with a public health leaflet on general hygiene and precautions regarding food, water supply, gas and electricity services and drainage. An information centre was set up in Long Road, where those returning home could obtain vouchers entitling them to free coal, bedding, furniture, disinfectant and cleaning materials.

No-one envied the people their task of 'getting back to normal'. No Lord Mayor's Fund could replace what the islanders had lost.

Fortunately, the island is now in a better position than it has ever been, for an advance warning system, with a network of communications, will go into action should there be any evidence of abnormal wind forecasts or freak tidal surges. Alarms from the central office (based in Norfolk) would go out to alert the services, county police, and coastal protection authorities. Ultimately the decision to alert the public to the danger of flooding in each area likely to be affected would be determined at a local level by the police and river board. The responsibility for, and method of, warning would, however, lie with the police.

The new wall which has been built around Canvey is a vast improvement on the design of the old stone-pitching; blockwork, steel sheet piling and concrete cap were used in the construction, and it was raised sufficiently high to prevent any overspill from the sea.

Regular observations and reports are made on the condition of the wall, and its relation to the slowly increasing sea level, with improvements recommended and acted upon periodically. However, vigilance against the elements must be continued, lest complacency sets in. A question which obviously arises from this is, 'Will it happen again?' In answer, all that anyone can really say is that, given the same set of circumstances again, it is highly unlikely that the same scale of devastation would occur. A quote taken from the speech by the Home Secretary at a debate following the 1953 floods sums this up: 'We have had a sharp lesson, and we shall have only ourselves to blame if we fail to profit from it'.

The First Coat of Arms

Armorial bearings were granted to the council on 5 January 1971. The arms were designed by the College of Arms, and depict symbols of local significance.

Wavy white lines on a blue background signify the River Thames that constantly laps the island's shores, whilst the snow white droplets allude to the early salt extraction. The island itself is fashioned as a green diamond lozenge, with the fat-tailed sheep that provided for the cheesemaking industry in the centre. Oyster shells stand at the four corners, referring to another past industry.

The sea walls are represented by the inner golden escutcheon; the inside is embattled to show the reinforcement of them. They are divided into seven equal parts, referring to the seven main drainage sluices that had previously been present.

Finally on the crest stands the Dutch cottage, today a museum, and the motto *Ex Mare Dei Gratia* meaning, 'From the sea by the Grace of God'.

Amusements and Recreation

It must be admitted that Canvey is no longer a paradise for wildfowl shooters and weekend shrimpers. The days of clambering over the rocks at low tide searching for a good harvest of mussels and winkles for Sunday tea are long gone.

Gone too are the boating-pool, the donkey rides and many old-fashioned but idyllic tea-rooms. No more the joyrides in an open plane as it winged its way high above Andrew's Grand Amusement Arcade. Gone too are the corrugated iron beach-huts and the black and white minstrel entertainers. However it is not all bad, for the community of islanders today are still keen on social life and are able to enjoy the kind of facilities of which our predecessors would have been jealous. There are cricket, rugby and football clubs for all ages, yachting, small boat sailing and angling, a golf course, swimming pool and running track, tennis, badminton and squash courts, weight training and fitness clubs.

There are clubs: theatrical, dance, political, disabled and musical to cater for all sections of the community, in addition to various hobby and self-help groups. Canvey is thus able to offer a community spirit which is second to none. B. A. Cave's *Official Guide to Canvey Island* of 1933 offers a quote on which to finish: 'A week in Canvey will do you more good than a fortnight elsewhere ... Come to Canvey Island'.

EX·MARE·DEI·GRATIA

Buried History

Swallowed by the sucking mud,
A history book in three dimensions,
Wooden bones of Viking ships,
Roman red hill clay inventions,
Buried by the sexton sea,
Carrying earth from England's core,
The river, with efficiency,
Levels out the shore.

Here men breathed the choking mist
Waiting for the sun to rise
To pan their salt, or wield their swords
In battle for this earthly prize.
Here peace settled silently
As native shepherds watched their flocks,
Here engineers kept back the sea,
With walls of mud and rocks.

The modern Island groans with rafts
Of buildings, covers of cement.
A concrete wall keeps out the sea,
Excludes its tidal sediment.
The mudflats ripple, newly drawn
By waves and currents every day,
Obliterating all the scorn
And grief of yesterday.

KATIE MALLETT

1. Built in 1618, the Dutch cottage was once advertised as a tea-room. It now houses a museum.

2. Another view of the Dutch cottage.

3. The second of the Dutch cottages dates from 1621, and stands in Haven Road. For much of its life it has been a private dwelling.

4. The Dutch cottage, now a museum, stands as one of the few reminders of Canvey's past.

5. The original place of worship on the island, the Dutch chapel, was demolished in 1712 and St Catherine's church built in its place; this was replaced by St Peter's in 1845. Another church, St Katherine's, replaced this in 1872.

6. St Katherine's church in the 1880s. This picture shows the poor state of repair of the churchyard and the boundary fence. The churchyard has now been extended on both sides and also to the rear.

7. St Katherine's church, at the turn of the century in a better state of repair.

8. This picture, which dates from 1901, shows St Katherine's church and the village school, both of which were wooden structures.

9. The village school in 1910.

IN THE NAME OF THE EVER BLESSED TRINITY AND FOR THE PROMOTION OF THE FAITH OF JESUS CHRIST THE MEMORIAL STONE OF THIS SCHOOL IS LAID BY HY HAYES, VICAR OF CANVEY ISLAND OCTOBER 19. A.D 1873.

10. The commemorative plaque celebrating the opening of the village school by the Rev. Henry Hayes on 19 October 1873. The Rev. Hayes was vicar of St Katherine's church and he did much for the welfare of his parishioners.

11.   A class of 1906.

12. A class of 1920 gathered outside the village school. If these are the happiest days of our lives, then where are all the cheery smiles?

13. This picture of 1889 shows workmen constructing the village pump. Before the introduction of the pump, residents of the island had to rely on water-butts for all their water supplies. The houses in the background of the picture still exist.

14. Thorrock Ales were on tap at the *Red Cow* in 1910, a favourite of the locals. Kipkabs Farm buildings can just be seen to the right and the village pump is in the foreground.

15.   The village pump served as a trough for animals, as well as providing the main water supply for the islanders.

16. *Ye Olde Red Cow* (later the *Red Cow*) situated in the village and destined to become the *King Canute*, following the floods of 1953, was a meeting place for villagers. This picture shows a view towards Northwick Corner.

17. There is no sign of the village pump in this 1950s picture of the village, but a lovely view of the Dutch cottage of 1621, and in the distance the *Red Cow*.

18.   Approaching the village from Canvey Road by Charfleets estate. On the left is the *Red Cow*, and on the right the village pump.

19.   A quiet Hole Haven Road. In more recent years, tankers along this stretch of road are a more common sight. The building on the right is the vicarage.

20.   Now known as Hole Haven Road, it was then more familiar as Sluice Road. In the left foreground stands the Dutch cottage of 1621; the house on the extreme left was occupied by the Andrews family. The village farm and the *Red Cow* public house can be seen in the distance.

21.   The coastguard station with the cottages in the background at Hole Haven. A sailor is seen manning the tower, and looks out over the estuary through his telescope.

22. The *Lobster Smack Inn* was host to prize knuckle fighting. It was not unusual to find a 'grudge match' in progress, due to a long-standing dispute. Supposedly the outcome of such a fight would settle the participants' disagreements once and for all. One such arrangement took place between Ben Court, a champion between the years 1838-45, and Nat Langham.

Thought to have originated from a family feud, Court, aged 42, took 37-year-old Langham to the 60th round on 22 September 1857. Though still on his feet, Langham had been knocked down no less than 59 times during the fight. It may have been Langham's sheer determination to continue fighting back at all costs that drew the match to an amicable conclusion at this stage, for they decided to end it by shaking hands and made up the quarrel.

Earning himself a title amongst islanders, Tom Sayers was pronounced the greatest of them all and habitually fought on Canvey. In a dramatic contest against Aaron Jones, on 19 February 1857, the fight was finally declared a draw by the referee when it became too dark to see. The count of the exact number of rounds on this occasion seemed to be vague. Some reckoned it lasted 62 rounds while others were just as unmovable in their belief that it was over 65. However, the return match caused no such dispute as Sayers won in the 85th round, when his opponent's seconds threw in the sponge, declaring him the outright winner.

A championship fight held on 16 June 1858 between Sayers and Tom Paddock lasted not nearly as long. In fact a mere 21 rounds drew the contest to its conclusion, Sayers emerging victorious. Of course, there was a considerable sum involved in this match, as, apart from the purse, there was also a 300 sovereign side-stake. This may have been reason enough to finish the bout speedily, but, just to show his opponent that he possessed a truly sporting nature, Sayers collected £30 amongst the spectators for the defeated Tom Paddock.

23. A naïve painting showing two Canvey policemen, *c.*1890. Policemen were not welcomed on the island and frequently during the summer months, when the resident policeman was called to assist at neighbouring Southend, all of Canvey was said to have turned out to cheer him on.

24. The principal farms of Canvey Island.

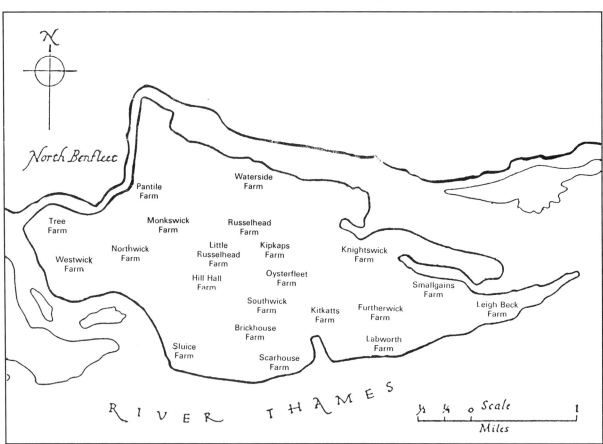

North Benfleet

Waterside Farm

Pantile Farm

Tree Farm

Monkswick Farm

Russelhead Farm

Northwick Farm

Little Russelhead Farm

Kipkaps Farm

Knightswick Farm

Westwick Farm

Hill Hall Farm

Oysterfleet Farm

Smallgains Farm

Southwick Farm

Kitkatts Farm

Furtherwick Farm

Leigh Beck Farm

Brickhouse Farm

Labworth Farm

Sluice Farm

Scarhouse Farm

RIVER THAMES

½ ¼ 0 Scale 1

Miles

25.   Scar House Farm was situated at the far end of Haven Road, approximately 500 yards from the *Lobster Smack Inn*. It is reported to have been the oldest farm on Canvey. Notice the thatched roofs of the barns.

26.   Leigh Beck Farm was bought by Frederick Hester for £2,000 in 1899-1900. It boasted one of the few artesian wells on Canvey and at one time residents bought their water from here, saving themselves a walk to the village.

27.   Milking time at Waterside Farm, 1928. Today the main buildng remains as a Castle Point Council depot. Unfortunately the barns have disappeared.

28.   A neighbour to the Dutch cottage, Hill Hall Farm stood on the Canvey Road, approaching Northwick Corner. The dual carriageway which now forms this part of the road was never considered when this picture was taken, and the fastest vehicle then was more than likely a horse and cart.

29. Sluice Farm stood about 200 yards to the rear of the *Lobster Smack Inn*. The *Lobster Smack* itself was once referred to as the *World's End*, and here we can see why.

30. Canvey was once covered with a large number of farms, and Island Farm, pictured here in 1928, was just one of them.

31. Walking about 100 yards from the *Haystack* public house in the direction of the seafront would have brought you to Furtherwick Farm, bordered by tall trees. On the same site today stands the Job Centre.

32. Knightwick Farm also made money by doubling as tea gardens. Notice the private well, looking like a windmill, in the centre of the picture.

33. Farmer White, seen here in retirement, ran a farm on Long Road, opposite Canvey County School.

34. Harvest time on Canvey meant a great deal of manual work as there were no tractors or mechanical aids to help, just horses and carts.

THE FERRY, LOOKING FROM CANVEY.

35. Heavily laden with a cargo of hay, this stackie is pictured in the creek making its way past the ferryman, who has pulled up at the causeway to wait for his next passenger. This picture dates from 1922.

36. Russellhead Farm House was built by Henry Theobald in 1928. Kath Wright (née Theobald) is pictured here c.1933 cradling Douglas Wright in her arms.

37. Nora Cook (subsequently Bishop) and her two sisters are seen here relaxing on the porch of the family's bungalow. Milk was sold to customers who called at the house. The bungalow faced onto the High Street. The Cook farm where cattle grazed is now Furtherwick Park School.

38. Standing 50ft. high at the entrance to the Winter Gardens, Hester's tower supported the show bungalow, where he would interview potential purchasers of his land. After his bankruptcy in 1905, the show bungalow was sold to a gentleman from London for his garden. The tower was declared unsafe, and on inspection it became apparent that local residents had removed sections of it for firewood; it was demolished in 1909.

39. Two ladies rest after walking through the botanical gardens of Hester's Winter Gardens. This picture dates from 1902.

40. Hester's mono-rail was able to carry 24 passengers across the island, in one of four horse-drawn carriages. The journey started at the Winter Gardens and ended at Shell Beach.

41. *The Kynoch Hotel* was built in 1900, close to the *Lobster Smack Inn*. The hotel was built by the Kynoch Estate Company of Kynoch Town (now Coryton). The building was constructed on land owned by the company, at a cost of £3,000. Many delays in building pushed the final costs to over £1,000 more than the original estimate. The hotel took four years to build. The first guests were business associates of the Kynoch Town Company. In 1907 a jetty was built near the hotel and both were put up for sale. No purchaser came forward. The *Kynoch* continued to operate until the Second World War, when troops stationed in the area took it over. It was later used as offices by the London and Coastal Oil Wharves, and then allowed to fall into disrepair. It was finally demolished in the 1960s.

42. Fishermen arriving at the Hole Haven landing stage with the day's catch.

43. This use of the two-storey structure known as the Lighthouse, in front of the *Oysterfleet* public house, has puzzled many people. It appears that it was built by an eccentric Captain Gregson as a home for his mother-in-law, in order to keep her out of his house! Sadly, this building has been demolished to make way for development.

44. The lake has a timeless history of its own. It dates back to Roman times and was used to reclaim salt from sea water. Dutch settlers built a wall around what is now called Small Gains Creek. It is thought that the lake was a continuation of the creek, since the discovery of a wooden sluice, which is now preserved in the Dutch cottage museum, gives weight to the theory. The lake was once used as an oyster bed, but now only fish and eels are to be found in it.

45 & 46.   The Girls' Rest Home or Girls' Bungalow, was opened by Miss Clara James on Whit Monday 1909. She believed that Canvey would provide the perfect atmosphere for the benefit of overworked and overstrained working girls. The bungalow on Lakeside path, near the *Oyster Fleet* public house, provided tranquil surroundings and the opportunity to relax.

47. Miss James also became involved in running the island, being a member of Canvey Council, a J.P., and a school manager. She was also founder member, president and trustee of Canvey Women's Institute and held a position with the First Canvey Girls' Life Brigade, attending displays regularly, and often acting as chairman.

48. Canvey Hall held religious services to cater for the residents of Leigh Beck.

49. The Canvey Hall outing of 1911.

50.   The terminus of Hester's mono-rail was known as Temple Bar. It also marked the development of the Winter Gardens.

51.   Powell's Stores stood at the end of Central Avenue, and catered for the residents of Winter Gardens. They were typical of many small stores at the time, selling just about everything imaginable. The Powell Company also had other premises: a popular restaurant at the rear of Benfleet station and a refreshment hut on the Canvey side of the bridge. This picture dates from 1925.

52. Looking down Winter Gardens path.

53. One of the seven sluices that existed to drain away the water from the island's dykes at low tide.

54.   Queues on the Canvey side of the causeway, waiting for the ferry boats to Benfleet. At low tide trippers would use stepping stones to walk across.

55.   A vehicle has been caught by the incoming tide. On the causeway passengers are getting into the ferry that will take them to the mainland.

56. In May 1930 Brigadier Colvin drove the first pile of the new bridge in an official ceremony. It was a momentous occasion for the island, but marked the end of an era for the ferryman.

57. Passengers from the ferry catch the bus at Waterside Farm that will take them to Canvey-on-Sea. This picture dates from 1928.

58. Taken in 1930 whilst the bridge was still under construction, this picture shows buses and lorries queueing to cross the creek as the tide recedes. All vehicles, especially trade deliveries, had to take into account the tide-tables to allow enough time for the delivery and return trip. Unfortunately some did not and were left stranded mid-stream.

59. A horse and carriage try to beat the advancing tide. Note the steam train in the background.

60. The Colvin Bridge opened to give priority to shipping, as seen here in 1934.

61. A public holiday was declared on the island in 1931 to mark the opening of the new bridge. Cubs, Scouts and Guides are seen here assembled for the occasion.

62. The Cash Stores, in Long Road, offered visitors a large tea garden with car park and camping ground, which was ideal for the outdoor holiday maker.

63. Jones' Stores at the corner of Craven Avenue and Long Road had previously been the Cash Stores. It was bought by Albert Jones who managed to build up a thriving business. It continued to prosper until the floods of 1953 and the retirement of Jones. This picture dates from 1928.

64. Mr. Matthews passes the time of day at the doorway of Matthew & Charles Estate Agents, Furtherwick Road. Note that when this picture was taken, in 1908, freehold land sold at £6 a plot.

65. The now redundant Castle Point District Council offices, photographed in 1992. Previously the left side of the block housed Canvey Fire Station and the right side the Ambulance Station. It has been suggested that the building be turned into a cottage hospital.

66.   Open day at the Fire Station for the families of Canvey firemen in 1957. This visit took place in Long Road, in the building which until recently was the council offices. Some firemen and their families pictured here still live on the island. From left to right (in the back row) they are: Arthur Edwards, Harry George, Ken McQuarry, George Blackwell, Harry Emmes, Sonny Blackwell, Frank Griffiths, Mick Saunders, Harry and Johnny Whitcombe and Geoff Barsby (senior).

67. A 1937 class from the William Read School.

8. This picture shows the William Read school before it was modernised. The school was named after its first headmaster, and was only the second school to be built on the island. Initially it served as a secondary school.

9. One of the more unusual bread delivery services to be seen on the island, in the 1950s, was that of Mr. Andrews on his three-wheel cycle. The author remembers that, as a young boy, he would lie in wait until Mr. Andrews had parked his cycle and knocked at a customer's door; he would then jump onto the unattended cycle and race off for a short ride, jumping off when Mr. Andrews gave chase.

70. One of Canvey's first motor buses meant bumpy journeys for passengers going to and from the causeway. Before this the journey would have been made by horse and cart. This picture dates from *c*.1925.

71. Canvey's very first ambulance of *c*.1930 was a far cry from the modern vehicle.

72. The first fire brigade on the island. This picture of 1929 shows the author's grandfather, front row, furthest right.

73. This picture of 1950 shows Canvey's firemen. The young boy on the right is Stanley Edwards. The driver is Harry George. The group also includes Ken Macquerie, Harry Whitcombe, Arthur Edwards and George Blackwell.

74.   The men of the Royal Artillery present a striking picture as they pose in 1938 outside the Heavy Coastal Battery Headquarters of the Territorial Unit based in Runnymede Road.

75.   Aubrey Stevens was a familiar figure, delivering bread around the island. He also founded, in 1977, the Canvey Historical and Conservation Society, becoming its first chairman.

76.   A loaded barge coming in to the Canvey Supply Company's wharf, *c.*1928. In those days bags of poilite cement would cost 2s. 3d. each.

77.   Canvey Supply Company delivers a window in Larup Avenue, long before the road was made up. When the weather was bad, carts fitted with runners instead of wheels were used to make journeys slightly easier.

78. A 1930s view down the High Street, showing the Canvey Supply Company's Clock Tower. The tower was covered during the war, since it provided a good identification point for enemy aircraft. It was demolished in 1967.

79. Canvey Supply Company's main depot, shown here before 1957. In that year fire swept through timber stored at the nearby wharf, destroying most of their premises. Fortunately the office building survived and the business was gradually able to build up again.

80. A view of the *Haystack* public house and Furtherwick Road, looking north. Notice the lack of shops.

81. In the early 1940s Agness Hepworth would sell a pint of shrimps for 1s. 6d. from the display of seafood outside Cockle Jack's. The shop is now an estate agent's next to Pollards at the *Haystack* corner.

82. Outside the *Haystack* public house in 1926.

83. For many years Vandersteen's, in Furtherwick Road, was the island's premier fish shop, serving wet and fried fish. The company prospered for a long time until the retirement of the proprietors. The premises today look quite different, but the shop is just as popular, trading as the Islander Fish Bar and Restaurant. This picture dates from *c.*1949.

84. Fielder bungalows in Craven Avenue. Residents then could not have known how busy this road would become once the dyke was filled in and the pathway made up.

85. The convent in Lionel Road. The sisters here were very enterprising, advertising frequently that they made coats, dresses, hats and fancy bags. Prices were also given on application for orders of homebakes, toffee, coconut ice and other confectionery.

86.   Before the caravan site developed at Thorney Bay, families would pay to pitch their tent on Colonel Fielder's Open Air Camp as this photograph of 1957 shows. Notice the three-sided 'luxury' ablutions.

87.   Thorney Bay Camp during the high season welcomed holidaymakers arriving in their thousands to pitch their tents. Amenities in the late 1950s amounted to a reception building, café and open-air theatre.

88.   The boating pool at Thorney Bay was popular with both locals and holiday-makers. The nearby beach hut which sold ice-creams, buckets and spades, etc., was owned by Lillian and Bertram Grout; the couple went on to own several very successful bakery outlets. Unfortunately the beach hut no longer exists.

89.   Waiting to catch a bus home after a trip to the beach. In the background is the Country Bay Club, now more familiar as the Goldmine.

90. Daytrippers park their cars and file across the bridge over the dyke to get to the beach. Note the absence of the Helter Skelter behind the Casino.

91. When it was first built in 1935, the Casino stood alone, in what is now Eastern Esplanade. Many couples met for the first time here, at the upstairs dance hall. Downstairs there were tea-rooms, a bar and amusements.

92. Built in 1851, the Chapman lighthouse stood as a warning to shipping for over a hundred years, before being demolished in 1957. Today a single bell-buoy marks the spot where the lighthouse once stood.

93. A trip in a pleasure boat around the Chapman lighthouse was a major attraction for visitors to the island.

94. The *Canvey Belle* was one of the island's pleasure boats, taking trippers as far out as the Chapman lighthouse and then back to the jetty.

95.   The stretch of sand seen here seems to have greatly diminished since this picture was taken.

96. Seen here in 1949, the old sea wall made an ideal picnic area for Canvey's many visitors. Note the motorbike combination to the left and the number of cars and people stretching into the distance.

97. The *Hotel Monico*, seen here in 1956, was a favourite dance hall for both residents and holiday-makers. Many locals me their future partners here.

98. If there was any doubt as to Canvey's popularity as a seaside resort, then this picture should dispel it.

99. The same area today, looking somewhat deserted.

100.   Another picture showing just how popular Canvey was in the inter-war years, as trippers wait to catch the bus home. No doubt the takings at the Café Rose, owned by the Thorne family, swelled on these occasions.

101.   When the tide was out the Chapman lighthouse (seen in the distance) could be reached on foot. The remains of the original Dutch sea wall can just be seen in the foreground. The modern sea wall stands approximately 100 yards further inland.

102.   Canvey was always a popular place for family outings and picnics. This picture, of 1911, shows the very low sea wall, the remains of Hester's jetty, and in the distance the Concord building.

103.   Local beauties enjoy a dip in the briny, 1925.

Proprietor: E. W. ANDREWS

104. Andrews' seafront amusement arcade was a major attraction for holiday-makers.

105. In Canvey's heyday visitors flocked down from London, excited by the number of seafront facilities. The boating pool, shown here in 1952, was just one of them. Later this was filled in to make way for a miniature train ride. Until recently the area was unused, but now a bandstand has been built.

106.   The corrugated iron beach huts at Shell Beach, seen here in 1924, appeared very flimsy, but at least they afforded bathers some privacy.

107.   In 1928 Canvey's seafront was full of places in which to eat, and Marlborough House was considered one of the finest. It was situated between Maurice Road and Keer Avenue. It also provided rooms to rent.

108. This became an all too familiar sight, in the years after the Second World War, as holiday-makers and day trippers flocked to the seafront. Notice the variety of vehicles that used to make the journey, and how close they were able to park to the old sea wall.

109. The people of Canvey have always loved fairgrounds, and here a part of Sutherlands Fair can be seen, next to the *Beach House Hotel*, at the end of Seaview Road.

110. Both locals and holiday-makers flocked to ride on Billy Wells' donkeys, which were to be found next to the Pierless Amusements. Seen on the back of the donkey are Ron Cox (at the rear) and one of his friends. Ron comes from an old Canvey family, and remembers many happy summers spend on the island.

111. Beach House and the little tea hut have long since disappeared and only fishermen and those with boats appear to use this area nowadays.

112.   Solidified concrete blocks salvaged from the wreck of the *S.S. Benmohr* are scattered on the shore in this picture of 1908.

113.   Joy-rides in this two-seater plane were very popular with holiday-makers in the pre-war years. The plane took off and landed in a field that was next to Andrews' Fair, by the Casino.

114. *Cox's Hotel and Café* was a popular venue with islanders for dances and social evenings.

115. The elegant *Ozonia Hotel*, with its thatched roof, stood where Seaview Court now stands. Unfortunately the hotel was never commercially successful, and many of its rooms were never occupied. On its ground floor was a small tea room, which provided lunches and teas at reasonable prices.

116. Hindles Road in the 1920s; notice the viewing balcony on the right-hand house. During this period a two-roomed furnished bungalow could be rented for about £1 5s. a week.

117. Sick animals were taken for treatment to the P.D.S.A. veterinary van which was at the Point area of Canvey.

118.　Green's Stores seen here in 1936 made every effort to tempt customers; their 'special offer' posters made a striking window display. Butter was sold at 1s per lb., peas at 3½d. a tin, cornflakes at 4½d. a box and shredded suet at 8d. per lb.

119. The Leigh Beck bus terminal has not always stood at the Point end of the island. In 1936 it was just past the *Admiral Jellicoe* public house, in the Seaview Road area.

120. Many bungalows on the island were converted into small businesses. Brown's Store, seen here in 1931, was one such business, selling everything from cotton thread to paraffin. It reverted to a private house in 1960, and has since been demolished.

121.   A gathering in the doorway of the Baptist Mission Hall, 1932.

122.   The residents of this bungalow ran a business hiring out ponies and traps.

123.   Bond's Stores, Leigh Beck, 1928.

124.   Chambers' Dairies and Fred Attwell's butcher's shop together occupied one of the very few buildings that had originally been built on stilts. After the road was lowered the building was adapted and is still in use today. A party balloon shop now occupies the premises which are not far from Small Gains Corner. It must have been quite perilous to cross the planks that formed the bridge to the shop.

125.   St Anne's church, which was reached by crossing a bridge over the dyke, has now been demolished, and a new church stands on the site.

126.   Canvey's first laundry service was based, at the time of this photograph, near Small Gains Corner; it later moved to the Knightswick area. It was obviously a well-used business, and one that the young Mary Webb (née Byron) protected whilst waiting for her father, Bill Byron, to reduce the pile.

127.   The Express Laundry delivery service. Whilst Bill Byron and daughter Mary were out making deliveries, Alice, Bill's wife, and his other daughter Gladys looked after the shop. Gladys and her husband John later took over the shop, but the introduction of self-service launderettes meant that the business became unviable.

28. Whittier Hall in the High Street was a popular meeting place for residents of the Leigh Beck area. The hall was used by Zoe Hammet's dance school and the Ladies Total Abstinence Society.

29. Zoe Hammet pictured in the 1930s. Zoe formed the island's first dance school. Among her many pupils was Queenie Grey (née Harris), who went on to become principal of Georgette's Juveniles, Dance and Stage School. Miss Hammet married a Rayleigh man, Charles Harding, but sadly she died in 1941, aged only 34.

130.   The Canvey Life Boys in Whittier Hall, taken in the 1930s.

131. Small Gains Club still exists today, at the rear of Tyremasters, Small Gains Corner. This picture was taken in 1926 before the road was lowered. The only entrance to the club was over a bridge.

132. The Orange Pips, pictured in 1936, were entertainers who performed at the Small Gains Club.

133. This picture of 1927 shows the road-works in High Street. During this time the road was lowered. The original High Street was the old sea wall, with the houses and shops on either side being supported on stilts. The lowering of the road meant that the duckboard bridges that had previously provided access to buildings were made redundant.

134. An early caravan parked on a plot of ground attached to a private bungalow, 1925.

135. Canvey's first indoor market was in the High Street, opposite Stevens' Bakery. This picture, taken in the 1920s, tempts customers with the offer of free admission.

136. The William Wilberforce bungalow. A resident of this bungalow grew so fond of it that he requested never to leave, even after death. His wishes were granted, for, when the bungalow was decorated following his death, it was believed that his ashes were poured into the pebble-dash mixture.

137. The Corner House was on Small Gains Corner and part of Small Gains farm. It was owned by Mr. Price Powell, an eminent local councillor and man of property; it was used by his chauffeur.

138. This is unrecognisable today as a spot where houseboats were moored and yachting took place. The creek was dammed in 1936, converting this area into open land. Recently it has been used for football pitches.

139. A look along High Street in 1932, showing the corner to Maurice Road on the right. The Granary building and several others further down the road still remain today.

140. Steve's Corner in Maurice Road was named after the owner of the general store.

141. A view down Maurice Road in 1912, looking towards the seafront. Notice the variety of buildings and the lack of garden flowers; also the unmade state of the road.

142. The Wireless Hospital, seen here in 1925, was in the High Street, opposite May Avenue. Like so many of the houses and shops in the area it was supported on stilts.

143. Clement's Dairies and their rival
Chambers' guaranteed the islanders
pure, rich milk, delivered to the door. On
site one could purchase dairy produce,
delicious ice-creams, and, of course,
Canvey Rock.

144. Mr. and Mrs. Went were the
popular proprietors of the Rendezvous
Club in Larup Avenue. Before it burnt
down, this was one of the island's more
successful social clubs.

145.   Once the main hall on Canvey, Bohemia Hall was erected *c.*1902. In its heyday it served the community well, acting as theatre, assembly room, conventicle, village hall, club room, cinema, headquarters of the Home Guard, and finally a factory. The Hall stood just before the approach of Small Gains Corner; today the area is covered by a housing estate. It may be remembered for its bazaars, Armistice services, stage performances and its showings of silent movies. Long before the Rio, Bohemia Hall was Canvey's first cinema. The quality of the picture was frequently poor – often stars such as Charlie Chaplin, Mary Pickford, Harold Lloyd and Tom Mix seemed to be acting through constant rain and snow storms due to the severe scratch marks on the film. For all its discomfort the Hall did have its own air conditioning – an aircraft propeller from the First World War, suspended from the ceiling. This novel idea was introduced by Mr. Henry Pettit who had served in the war. Henry was responsible for the running of the cinema and the hiring of films. The early silent movies had captions underneath and these did not always run in time with the picture. The showing of a film set in the 17th century, *Captain Blood*, provided a fine example of this – in a scene where the fiercesome, swashbuckling Captain was giving chase to another sailing ship, the text read the command 'Full steam ahead'. However the amusement that this caused ensured that the film drew big audiences.

Local businesses had their advertisements printed on the safety curtain so that they could be read before and after the show. Some of the island's more daring children crept in through the back wall to watch their favourite films, and Henry Pettit was once heard to call upon the audience for volunteers to help throw the children out. Today big cinemas with luxury seating and high quality blockbusters are taken for granted, but just as much enjoyment was to be had in Bohemia Hall.

146.   Since its opening in 1956, Newlands Holiday Camp has seen many changes. It opened as a simple, council-run tent camp. In 1958 Jack King bought the camp and the first of a number of chalets appeared. Today, still under the same ownership, the camp, renamed King's Holiday Park, has a swimming pool, mini zoo, shops, club house, children's and public bars, a diverse entertainment programme, seasonal fishing in the lake, and a large number of residential as well as holiday chalets, and plenty of space for caravans. To quote from a company brochure, the camp offers visitors, 'A Holiday of a Lifetime'. King's Holiday Park is the island's foremost holiday site, welcoming thousands of visitors every year. The picture shows a caravan entering the camp in the early 1960s. The building on the right is now better known as Steve's Radio Cars.

147.   The camp shops at King's Holiday Park in the 1960s.

148.   The Nutshell Café offered a variety of meals at very reasonable prices. The picture shows Mr. Pitt to the left with two other members of his family. The Nutshell stood in the High Street where Del's Card Shop and The Book Shop are now.

149. Typical Canvey bungalows in the 1920s. Unmade roads, no street lighting but plenty of space. These were probably used by Londoners as holiday homes.

150. The Hazel Tea Rooms, in 1924, again with the familiar duckboard bridge across the dyke. This building later became Hazel Fisheries and was run by the Hopton family, until a compulsory purchase order was placed on it, to allow for a wider road and the Knightswick Centre.

151. Many curious shoppers turned out when the Alterman Arcade opened for the first time in 1955. The arcade stood on the site of the Knightswick Centre.

152. Knightswick Road, looking towards the town centre and Lakeside Corner. On the right now stands Flickers Hair Studio and Ware Bros., and to the left is Barclays Bank.

53. Cherry Stores in Central Wall Road was one of Canvey's first private lending libraries. The first public library was opened in September 1947.

154. The Central Club was one of the many social clubs on the island during the inter-war years.

155. Furtherwick Road in 1948-49, showing the London Co-operative Society Ltd. The shop comprised bread shop, greengrocer, and grocery store.

156.   Furtherwick Road looking towards the *Haystack* in 1955. Chambers Dairies is next door to the Rio cinema. Notice that the road is much narrower than it is now.

157.   The flat-roofed building adjacent to the bungalow served as St Katherine's Lodge for Freemasons. In 1939 the owner of the property was Mr. Chambers, the chairman of Canvey Urban District Council, it was later bought by Mr. Charles Hollingberry, both men were well-known local figures. The building, which is situated in Furtherwick Road still stands, but has been extended beyond all recognition.

158. Pictured here are 'Uncle Sam's Canvey Minstrels', very popular entertainers of the 1930s, on one of their 'Whitenights'.
This picture is unusual because the group were usually photographed blacked up.

159. This look-alike Dutch cottage was built in May Avenue, and served as a tea-room.

60. A walk with the baby was a pleasant outing, especially when the sloes were in full bloom. This picture dates from 1912.

161. An aerial view of the Thameside Crescent/North Avenue council estate. The floods here were not high as in other areas, but the residents were still evacuated from the island.

162.   Despite the flooding, approximately 1,000 people insisted on staying on the island. To cater for their needs Jones' Stores on the corner of Craven Avenue remained open.

163.   A bird's-eye-view of the damage caused by the floods in 1953.

164. This picture, taken when most people had been evacuated from the island, shows Craven Avenue under water, with a single rowing boat tied to a lamp post.

165. Caught by the floods, Mr. Liddiard, the well-known proprietor of Green Glades Restaurant and his own dancing school, improvised with a few steps of his own! He used his kitchen chairs as a means to get to the safety of higher and drier ground.

166.   During the floods members of the services and many volunteers helped to move people to safety.

167.   The sign for Hindles Road may be seen over the top of a wooden bench, just visible through the flood waters. In this area the sea level reached some of the rooftops. Many residents were forced to spend the night on the roof before being rescued.

168.   A single rowing boat makes its way down Denham Road at the height of the floods.

169. A child is transferred from a rescue boat to an army lorry. During the floods police, ambulances, firemen and members of the services worked together. This picture was taken in North Avenue, where the author was born. His father was the one in the boat who managed to raise a smile.

170. Volunteers and members of the services worked side by side to repair the breach in the sea wall following the floods.

171. The stuffed bear tied outside Jones' Stores was already a familiar sight to islanders. During the floods it 'carried' a sign reading 'Canvey will rise again'.

FREEHOLD
SEASIDE PLOTS

THE 'OLD DUTCH ISLAND'

2ɔ Miles only from Fenchurch Street   Good Train Service   Cheap Rates

F. W. B. HESTER

Every WEDNESDAY and THURSDAY

500 PLOTS

OF VALUABLE

FREEHOLD BUILDING LAND

Oyster Fleet & Shell Beach Estates, Canvey-on-Sea, Essex,

This Land will in the course of a very short period greatly increase in value, and at the present time affords a splendid opportunity to both large and small buyers.   Several of the Estates are already developing

WINTER GARDENS, ELECTRIC RAILWAY, PIER, Etc.

Every facility is offered to Visitors and Holiday Seekers

BUNGALOWS and REFRESHMENTS on very reasonable terms by the
WEEK, MONTH or QUARTER

Bracing Air.   Good Fishing, Shooting, Boating & Bathing.

10 per cent gives immediate possession

Free Deeds. .. Easy Payments.

FREE RAILWAY VOUCHERS to attend the Land Sale and
View the Estates can be obtained of the Auctioneer.

F W B HESTER, 145, Fenchurch Street, E.C, or
The VENDOR, Estate Office, Canvey-on-Sea, Essex, and also at the
No 4 Platform Barrier Fenchurch Street Railway Station